QUODLIBET

✺

CHLOË JOAN LÓPEZ

QUODLIBET

✻

CHLOË JOAN LÓPEZ

✻

NEW MICHIGAN PRESS
TUCSON, ARIZONA

NEW MICHIGAN PRESS
DEPT OF ENGLISH, P. O. BOX 210067
UNIVERSITY OF ARIZONA
TUCSON, AZ 85721-0067

<http://newmichiganpress.com/nmp>

Orders and queries to nmp@thediagram.com.

Copyright © 2009 by Chloë Joan López.
All rights reserved.

ISBN 978-1-934832-18-9. FIRST PRINTING.

Printed in the United States of America.

Design by Ander Monson.

Cover photo © Alex Bramwell | Dreamstime.com

CONTENTS

Curled with Amalthea's Horn   1
A Wedding Ring, I   2
Georgette   3
Hundred-Handed & Convivial   4
A Wedding Ring, II   5
Today or Tomorrow   6
Critique by Tiger   8
Megan Dilligent   9
A Wedding Ring, III   17
The Dark Ages   19
The Tragedy of Kinds   21
The Airfield   23
I Cannot Say That When I Saw You
   You Did Not Look Like a Lover   25
We Think This, but Never Is It Seen   27
Grandmaster Michael & Grandmaster June   29
Life of an Effigy   32
A Wedding Ring, x   34
The Colegio   35
Rounding the Stairs   44

Acknowledgments   46
Notes   47

CURLED WITH AMALTHEA'S HORN

In it is supposed to be enough: the peach
That rolls from the drive to the lawn
Is a planetary sphere, a cranium, a world,

A social circle, a globular eye,
A man's testis and a woman's
Whole body—but do you believe it?

Narrow your field of view by minutes
Of arc, until peoples and personalities
Shade into each other, and fabric marks

Neither society nor space-time, but the stained
Shirt whose minute rip you envy—and fear.
Until one thing only is the one thing.

We leave these doll's heads—painted
Indelibly enough for teeth and lips
To be made out, even after years—to bob up

Eyeless, on some waste-washed shore.
Bill says that metaphor is a lie:
America, a stand-in for a stuntman,

Encompassing as much and as little
As its noisome beaches, as
The body and its tumor, the diseased

Mind and its inspiration,
As—more is insult. Nothing more.

A WEDDING RING, I

A wedding ring is a trap. Or, to be precise, a snare: a wire wound round a trickling neck. The red ribbon centipedes down, against marsupial consent, to join the cinch at the waist. Pawning off—the rounding error, the unskimmed. The above-prime rate, as marginal return, whispered off the trader's slate.

A wedding ring is forfeiture that asks, "What epsilon ever comes close enough *not* to erupt from dark? In what seemly verdigris do pennies cloak themselves, that the audit might slip overhead?" A question cannot be concurred.

When surfeit & certitude convene, we grant, the calipers relax. The laser light & lens both begin to drift, & those lovers, wave-function & time-series, begin a dance. The ribbon proceeds, down belly, to trace a velvet inseam. No call, no run—just an anklet turn *en pointe*.

Two trackers, working backwards, will sniff the red dots & the earth. "This," says one, "is emboldened."

GEORGETTE

If you come to meet me for coffee
    I will wear a georgette skirt
        And if you leave the television on
I will look for the lighter you left here
If you teach me "thank you" in Arabic
    I will sing into the telephone
        And if you let the hallway fill with drafts
I will send you a pressed violet

For whenever I find myself writing a check
    The eraser has paused against your lips
        And whenever I find myself smoking unfiltereds
The Jetta has idled at the end of your block
For whenever I find myself chopping shallots
    The cookbook has opened to the page with your handwriting
        And whenever I find myself boarding the ferry
Dioramas have proffered your forthright questions

But little by little
    The cream curdles and the sugar dissolves
And little by little
    The cigarettes ash and the cars run rich
As little by little
    The galleries close and the sea swells ashore

HUNDRED-HANDED & CONVIVIAL

Into the rock are cut
many rungs.

                                        Paul is a man
                                   who licks his palms

Nieces and nephews
cannot attest

                                  when not at his desk.
                                        Zeal or lust

to the governance
of days.

                                    can be misplaced
                                  or rephrased. He begins

For your benefit
a story may be

                                           the climb right
                                      where he left off,

offered. Take it to tell
at lunch over

                                    crossing the gap
                                  like a hundred-handed

wine and pleasantries.
Solitary choices

                                monkey, suspended in air
                                  but clenching tightly,

are, in any case,
pitted like cherries.

                                         unwilling to fall.

A WEDDING RING, II

A wedding ring is ceramic, a heat shield air-dropped from the Migraine—from her curls & eyes. A wedding ring plunks, then skitters, then caroms like a ball bearing let fly upon the leaf or the wheel.

The wind drawn through it drives forth the ghosts, the *gusanos*—eccentric scourges all—with a howl.

And the howl becomes a string on which the concerto plays, through which the wave crests thread. Until, at last, with the devilry in frothing retreat, the sonoluminescence, stamped out in O's, gleams in black imagination.

A wholeness foretold in blackness, in tempest, & your voice goes out among the dire din, & goes out—invoking the droplets, the deluge belayed, the grim gift that it once was—leading the imps & tricksters, Gorgons & satellites to pause and turn to see what echoes, what reflects.

TODAY OR TOMORROW

It could be Wednesday. It could
be Tuesday. It could be midnight.
It could be three goldfish in the garden
pond. Or it could be three carp—
with an eddy, they are gone.

It could be the half-
light of autumn on the Arctic
Circle. Or of spring
on the Antarctic Circle. They could be perfect
circles, but they could be ovals,
uneven and ready to cleave.

It could have been fifteen cherry
petals, wafting on updrafts, submitting
to the ascendant summer sun; or
could have been
(likely was) a sun
twice reflected,
stopping sound, shedding ash.

¡Corazón!—We could have sampled muscat,
settled under elm trees, hid
from the dapples of the trefoil sun:
I would have liked to arrange pink
apple blossoms, just to be blessed—
to set thirteen in a ring at your feet.

Or we could have made dashes
from poplar to poplar, while
miniature rain drizzled, while the knowing
chrysanthemums nodded:
I would have liked you to catch hold
of my wrist, to leave your wet

thumbprint just so on my lip. It could be
the multitudinous ocean basin, dark
and teeming, striving
stemlike for the light. It could be the stony
coastline, acquiescent and limning,
assenting to the spray.
It could be both (yes,
both) in the cyclone of nightfall.
It could be the whirling orrery overhead.

The unknown fish reappear in the water,
eyes blank. I sit at the pool's edge, dip
three fingers in—and look away, singing. Goldfish
might well
have fled from the ripples
and song, but *koi*,

koi know when to linger, could
be lingering even now, listening
and rapt. It could be that way—it could be
tomorrow. It could be today.

CRITIQUE BY TIGER

after May Swenson

May my defiance perish in your jaws, succumb
as in a dream on the grassy nights
you stalk. May I be overcome
by shredding, tender fury,
if I should dare. If I should sleep, please, breathe your bites

along my cassocked shoulders: leave a mark. Your hide
spread its slat-stenciled tapestry
across my face, the bones inside
withheld from any query
by muscles undulating under muscle. See,

my manuscripts are marmalade aflame, my ink
awash, with its gamy mollusk scent.
The claim form that read "Wild beast (extinct),"
denied, despite my penury,
your diamond eye: the way, without consent,

you patterned me. For you, the closets are gorged with kills,
the furniture has gone askew,
and my twenty favored words lie still
along the curve of your worry
teeth. You could splinter them. I want you to.

MEGAN DILLIGENT

I.

Seven past
twelve. The silence I hear

still is not hers.

II.

Dilligent mows riverbanks
three times fortnightly. In
cases that move her to mow

in the evening, the bright
mud, a shining cradle-cap,
smells to her of a memory

of torrents, torrents
and flooding—

flooding whose greenstick
currents snapped,
whose freshwater urgency chilled
like darkcore. Even still,

she leaves here bearing
the mottlings and pinpricks left
on her hard (and soft) palate

by desolate, unmarked
weeks of inhaling runoff

and silt. She waits a bit, kills
the motor, adds some oil—lights a cig.

III.

Whenever she comes to have
mown in the morning, Dilligent

makes time to linger
and watch. Her slate Zippo
tingles, stowed

in her dark locket,

as twenty-two million
gray-green blades
commence a vegetative labor—
to collect the morning

freshness, her stillness,
and the light
of the culminating
sun. Collected and

crushed, like petals
beneath pestles,
they thicken, thicken,
thicken the leaves. The

baby grass
bristles in
precisely.

Then she lets herself breathe
in deeply, as the daybreak

dew reprises itself
on her dark, bare, muscled
back. At noon, the sun

stops.

IV.

Twelve times out
of seven hundred, I know,
she even must mow
at midnight. The myrmidon

riverbanks will hear
her approach, and will have hidden,
hidden themselves with leaves.

Far away, the sorrowing
cottonwoods will low
with—and long for—the wind. Fish
silhouettes will leap and gulp
at the breath-laden air—yet

still she'll push.

V.

She told me why, once, why,
why she will
push
that ramshackle mower
back and across
three times over—the fields

at stony standstill, the moon
glowering—and still I know

she will. She will.

Barely roused,
one midnight, I
heard her
say it, as I watched
her knot her
hair in braids. "Look,"

said Dilligent, dark

eyes roiling, "wool's warm
plenty, and this coat
fits snug. At night,

the grass may stand
still, but
the clouds lean close.
The chill's

in the air but my blood
beats hot, deep
in the lungs. You're soft

and don't understand—" she kissed
me then (tasting

of
cloves) "—but if

I stay late
enough the drizzle
may come." Come kiss me

again, my Megan.

VI.

Still, come those violent
midnights, I'll miss her:
I'll finger my opposite
locket, soon to dream
of cottonwoods deluged, deluged
by shadows and salt—

soon to imagine I see
her, a woman with inlays
of granite, squinting, barely
smiling, meeting the mist

and the moistness, giving
her face, sun-
worn, for the droplets
to kiss.

A WEDDING RING, III

A wedding ring is the gavel bruise leveled by the tribunal. Or left by the box of knobs hurled in tumult at the pane. In a splatter of paint chips, in a scourging.

Judgment, *nolo*, *cola*, rouged—the panelists' lips purse, their eyes dragged down ashen, as each intones entreaties, brash resorts to untoward stone:

> The jilted princess & her whited anemia preside, with doffed tiara: a squirming stillbirth on the bench;

> The child with ears for eyes & no memory of, no talent for what that means;

> The ugly one—beset by scars, by lopsidedness, blotches, by cartilage & fat—absently paring mangoes;

> The love-slaughtered, whose dulled eyes sneer—first splayed, then blued—between motions to recess;

> A supine raft of cannon fodder;

> The disgraced pervert with skull worn through, who tries clicking clefts together, throughout arguments, in hopes doctored tumblers can throw the bolt;

And the novitiate, slender & shorn, alternately auguring with the scurrilous glass and dowsing with a sieve, late of the public inquiry that tried the Great Omentum.

Squalls of bested lenience is all they have, all they have to impart, save adjournment, & a moot reading into record of default handed down.

THE DARK AGES

How can I tell you
how the dark ages began?
How the knife slipped
in from behind to tear
through the kidney?
"How prescient she was!"
they surely are saying,
"How fatal and how doomed!"

How can I begin,
recalling that last day,
whose spring sun was striking
and clear, even in the chill? The air
not even bracing, and in it, no cloud hanging?

Those who claim to feel warmth
in X-rays are malingerers and wrong—
make no mistake.
But we believe in invisible things,
the whispers in the films,
because of what will be shown,
and what is to come.

In the cryptic hour,
a singer sings of going deaf,
as if noiselessness were what
would calm his sorry soul, but only
because loss promises to rush in,

drowning everything out.
And it will. But then, in the voice
of the text, sorrow
will resume.

Ask the seer his name,
his nationality, again
and again, and again, and not
because you want to know.
For you, he will split
a bird in this mutual rite
and warble out some hunch.

The wreck of the hopeful heart—
Can the secret abide in caves,
in jawbones or amber,
while hope founders and goes down?

The seer mumbles, not to himself, but the sky.
The singer's voice aims at heaven, but falls back, striking him.
And I can mouth lines
only about the sun, the spring,
and always cooling air.

THE TRAGEDY OF KINDS

for Eva Johanna

In the monsoon, dreams
are flocks in migration. Bodies become

landmarks and breezes, and even
bird-minds are bracketed and glossed.

In wakefulness, orphaned
shadows are heard fluttering
down to pick the locks
against night's backdrop,

an incidental music becomes possible
with no one to bat them away:

> song—
> heard hummed in the throat,
> hung in darkness from the window seat
>   across to the door left ajar.

In the Madagascar wet, wanting
not water but salt, a moth, unlike the many
who live on tears, must work up
   a toothed tongue,
   a straw to tuck beneath the lids
   of an eye it dares not wake

as it sups the secrets
    of the leached-out earth.

In the forest
of the agile
    with no daylight place to land,

what is shut must be spread
    apart by ornamented barbs,
    by ringlets
    in sketchbooks always left unshown:

    a miniature made
    of the lifting of folds,

    with no attempt to glean
who ought to fly and who ought
to sleep.

Miners do not consult their mountains,
nor do great powers warn
    the islanders. And again, livestock
    swish their tails across
the haunches of their continent,

in the tragedy of kinds.

Survival may be theft,
    but never so patient or so numb.

THE AIRFIELD

The Aviator calls it "Heaven for Planes." As the clouds fall in, filing themselves into gills, into magnanimous stripes of sky, the Aviator is moved to point up at them. Within them whirl perfect touchdowns of thought, three-point notions taxiing into rows.

But here on the tarmac, I am waving my arms, with lights and painted lines pulled up in cupfuls, cradled where each trajectory now lies. And tracers and contrails give lavender light.

This woeful expanse—I cannot bring it around. Nothing left to launch, not even hangars. Not even divots, first gouged by debris and wreckage, later by my fingers and nails. The pockmarks have lain insensate for well nigh years on end. There's nothing they match. I know: I've turned the map over, again and again. Cockpit recordings flutter past in unheard strands.

The airfield is an island, and I am marooned. The clouds unjustly float on. Potshots are not so fun anymore; the crisscross strips, a faint, crabgrassed abstraction.

The abstraction is mine. The abstraction is this: that in a hopscotch push to the coast, a demented fleet admiral will lob a depot dream. Airborne engineers will be inserted on lilacs, with cache-and-pipeline plans. Blacktop will steam and rivets run. The flurry will continue in precision and haste, until—first stirring seismically, then lolling, then turning, then rising with all the ambition of flight, then pivoting upward, then lumbering, then with a beacon's towering—my body regains its untoward height.

Instead, with the pinging of coins, the spiteful clouds have begun to rain.

I CANNOT SAY THAT WHEN I SAW YOU YOU DID NOT LOOK LIKE A LOVER

But I fear our
palms, held
distant, hold more than
palms pressed
close. Desire is capacitance. Usually. In my case

it is needlework and pain—*that*
is capacitance—and a glowing
pinpoint that threatens
to defect, desire mere field
lines gathered alongside.

Wafers of distrust wedged between.

Between
the planetarium and its dome, I have
finally learned.

Learned to savor. Learned to dwell. Learned to live on
the nourishment of glass
beads and air that leave
only texture on the tongue. To leave the skin
an unfurred cloth that weeps
its charge. To harbor only untried faiths.

Poised above the star-
gazers' stiffening
necks, amid dialects
and loss, I am reckoned
as among the supergiants: We decay,
or arc to ground.

WE THINK THIS, BUT NEVER IS IT SEEN

I live in a rocky niche, sheltered
from the wind, but never
quite dry, where the sun shines in only
three times a year.

Suspicious of comfort,
of course you live atop rocks. Desperate
to survive, of course
you remain perched there. Like

a sunstruck bird, you perch and sing.
From below, I hear the shouts of an unseen
man: Elijah, in waiting, elsewhere
along the analemma: not even the sun

sees us both at once. There is a word
for this plight in his
language, I am sure of it, one
of the things he shouts:

like *Nothing ever is erased.* And *We think this
but never is it seen.*

Even cold water runs a course
as much as it swirls.
Instead what we see are friends
who turn away, never seen

to age. We judge the shortening
tendons by how
hands claw into fists. We see
landscapes not nearly

so tall as we remember them, colors
not nearly so rich,
as they bleach into noon. What have they
to do with us, our

tremored grasp? Elijah is howling
again, surely from want
of knowing. And from the sun.
I do not know what

language he speaks, but in his clamor
I have come to hear:
Deluge. Delectation. Lift.

GRANDMASTER MICHAEL & GRANDMASTER JUNE

for Mike Ryan

Grandmaster Michael would
bicycle
fervently, gingerly
turning the corners of
flowerbeds.
The road paved
itself for
Grandmaster Michael, &
deftly
was he
always moving.

Grandmaster June would
wait
among irises, & would turn
over the world
through the gaps between
stems. Raindrops would
light
like birds in her
hands,
on her outstretched
arms, as
the sun smiled
down on
Grandmaster June.

On Sundays Michael would
turn
a sharper curve, & would
reverently file through
the gathered-in
rows of
lilies & peas. The
raindrops would
be
expectantly still,
perched
on the stretches
of leaves &

petals. June would sleep
still
behind curtains
of sunlight & shadows, &
sometimes would
smile.
(The raindrops would spatter.)

When Michael had gingerly
slowed
to a stop, June would
awake & stretch out
her hand
through the sheltering
stems
guarding her face.

Her fingers would
pierce
the gaps between spokes
in the bicycle
wheel
that had come to a
reverent
halt. Deftly they would
curve
around the

vanadium—
radiant,
cold &
sharp.

LIFE OF AN EFFIGY

The flora escape me.
    No rain can be carried
to its intended,
                      even

resorting to cannulae in throats
    open for singing.
I have turned the
                      bedclothes

down. And bales
    of weather, the clouds,
are sheets of
                  newsprint

pressed and ungummed. Sicknesses in bird
    life—hollow shafts
of feathers in preened
                          rows—

are not the ability to spell, to stack
    downstrokes and minuscules
between shims.
                When

slaking comes, my skin will gleam,
    but inward, within the warm
wet, proof against the
                          glaze,

and proof to appraisal—I am made mask
   and shawl, quickened, like a kachina
attested on the last mesa:
>   *He'e'eh*

who ran, her hair half whorled, half
   strewn along unwilling,
from her bridal toilette, to sink into the
                     glyph

of war. Painted-to-be and gutted,
   we dry.
When the imperious sun
               leaflets

us again, and the arroyos still,
   I will lie, sifted
with the clay and, like it,
               blank,

curled by dryness into scrolls.

A WEDDING RING, X

Without it there were hives

of wasps. Now, in a cave

ground by wind, steadily,
                              into a rock, I can sit

cross-legged in the cream & unstirred yellow

of sandstone.
                Worn, hard-won, (hiding

   someone I knew I could not marry)

& centuries old, ventifacts suffice.

   (A dry rage mouth turned down to the floor.)

It is not refusal

   but unwillingness to trade.

THE COLEGIO

I.

It began in a New England town, when he
and his sister took turns, each pretending
to expel the other
from their grade. That town in September

is rusted, all meandering roads
converging to a spire: the Unitarian church.
A boy and a girl, they had never

before been allowed in the same Sunday school.
As penance they alternate:
authority and the branding of humiliation.

II.

In his country, when snow
piles atop the walls, the trash
heaps and stacks of magazines
are just more color. His sketchbooks,

taken as evidence, will reveal
the honeycombs of the city,
its pockmarks, pitted bricks, apartment
blocks, and rutted roads. His people
are expert conservators, trading

in painted metal and plaster, those things
that will be beautiful after
they have been forgotten,
after they have ceased to work.

III.

Once the season changes, I pull back
the tarp to rake
away the layer

of ice that crusts there. It ices
over whenever it is allowed
to still. This duty was made

easier by knowing
she sat reading on the other side
of the sliding door.

IV.

The root of the idea came in just
such a winter, as he stood preparing
to reenter the restaurant. The *guitarrón*'s
low notes spread their warmth, one

befitting the haze of summer. But warmth
felt distant then from where he stood among the deep
footprints, the pick-up trucks, and all

the dirty ice. Only one tonic
for winter: restoration, and to pretend
it was the only place he'd known.

V.

Those who know of it know
that the Colegio was
the site of no government. It is

only stone walls
run outside a courtyard; the southwest
corner of the keep.

They enclose the perorations only
of breezes and brackish water. But together
with the marked

floorplan of neighboring ruins, they are memory's
capitol. They appear on all
the currency.

VI.

On the bus back from the lab, I watched
the riders and their
struggle to cover their unease. They pretended,
not that they did not
hear the radio

news, but that they did not understand. Uprising
reminds
many too much
of defeat. The correspondent's voice
loomed over their abdication.

VII.

And how his sister stood agape
outside the graphic
arts library, reading words
from the screen but unable
to watch. "Nothing," she later said
she thought, "prepared

him for this." She touched
the painted moldings. She thought
of red leaves.

VIII.

In his cell, he was found

a changed man. His swanlike

neck, the soft smile

on his face. His cut-straw hair hung

evenly above

his pale, now boyish cheeks. This face

IX.

continues to confound the newsmen who transmit
it to my study at the end
of every June, as if for my signature, even years
after his sister has gone, in mad

reprisals for their disbelief. In the footage,
he smiles because he has forgotten
everything. He will give
no one up. The next year the tourist crowds
will return. But in that moment

the blessed sky has
been hauled down, brought
near enough to hear.

ROUNDING THE STAIRS

for Miranda Gaw

We meet so high up that our accompanists are planes. From the observation deck, we watch them spiral in both directions with lighted wing tips, pink and green. Since there is nothing to say there is nothing we say.

In Manhattan, stairwells are bridges. You may ascend and descend with one hand always on the wall. You may. You may watch your shoes the whole way down: canvas shoes, if you will, in pink and green.

Each month means a higher floor and a narrower tower. By year's end we face each other across the circular inner railing, on a reverse crow's nest with hardly a place to stand. The wind speaks between us, and the planes, in long orbits.

Were there cards to punch, I would punch them, and slip them into boxes of saltines. Were there cartridges or turntables, we might splice in an earphone—and yet make the broadcast. Instead, in a tapping, I hear some kind of grasping, wrapped with brown paper: a packet destined to be hid in a drawer.

So high up, the antenna is sharp, and surely will be piercing. It will be my hand—pierced—or it will be yours.

ACKNOWLEDGMENTS

Grateful acknowledgment is made to the following publications where some of these poems first appeared.

"Megan Dilligent": *can we have our ball back?*

"Critique by Tiger" and "We Think This, but Never Is It Seen": *DIAGRAM*

"Georgette": *Georgia State University Review* (now *New South*)

"Today or Tomorrow": *Mississippi Review*

"The Dark Ages": *Spoon River Poetry Review*

Special thanks to Lucie Brock-Broido, Miranda Gaw, the fine poets of the Off-Season crew, the Massachusetts Cultural Council, and the Cultural Organization of Lowell.

NOTES

"Critique by Tiger" is inspired by May Swenson's poem, "Poet to Tiger."

In "The Dark Ages," the singer is Alan Sparhawk of Low in their song "When I Go Deaf."

"The Tragedy of Kinds" is based on a short article, "Moths Drink Tears of Sleeping Birds," that appeared in *The New Scientist*.

"The Airfield" echoes a line from Werner Herzog's documentary film *Little Dieter Needs to Fly*.

"We Think This, but Never Is It Seen" alludes to the events in 1 Kings 19:9-14.

Originally from New Mexico, CHLOË JOAN LÓPEZ earned an M.A. in poetry from the Writing Seminars at the Johns Hopkins University. Her work was recognized in 2006 by the Artist's Grant program of the Massachusetts Cultural Council. She lives in Somerville, Massachusetts.

❋

NEW MICHIGAN PRESS, based in Tucson, Arizona, prints poetry and prose chapbooks, especially work that transcends traditional genre. Together with DIAGRAM, NMP sponsors a yearly chapbook competition.

DIAGRAM, a journal of text, art, and schematic, is published bimonthly at <http://thediagram.com>. Periodic print anthologies are available from the Del Sol Press or the New Michigan Press.

❋

COLOPHON

Text is set in a digital version of Jenson, designed by Robert Slimbach in 1996, and based on the work of punchcutter, printer, and publisher Nicolas Jenson.

www.ingramcontent.com/pod-product-compliance
Lightning Source LLC
Chambersburg PA
CBHW031433040426
42444CB00006B/784